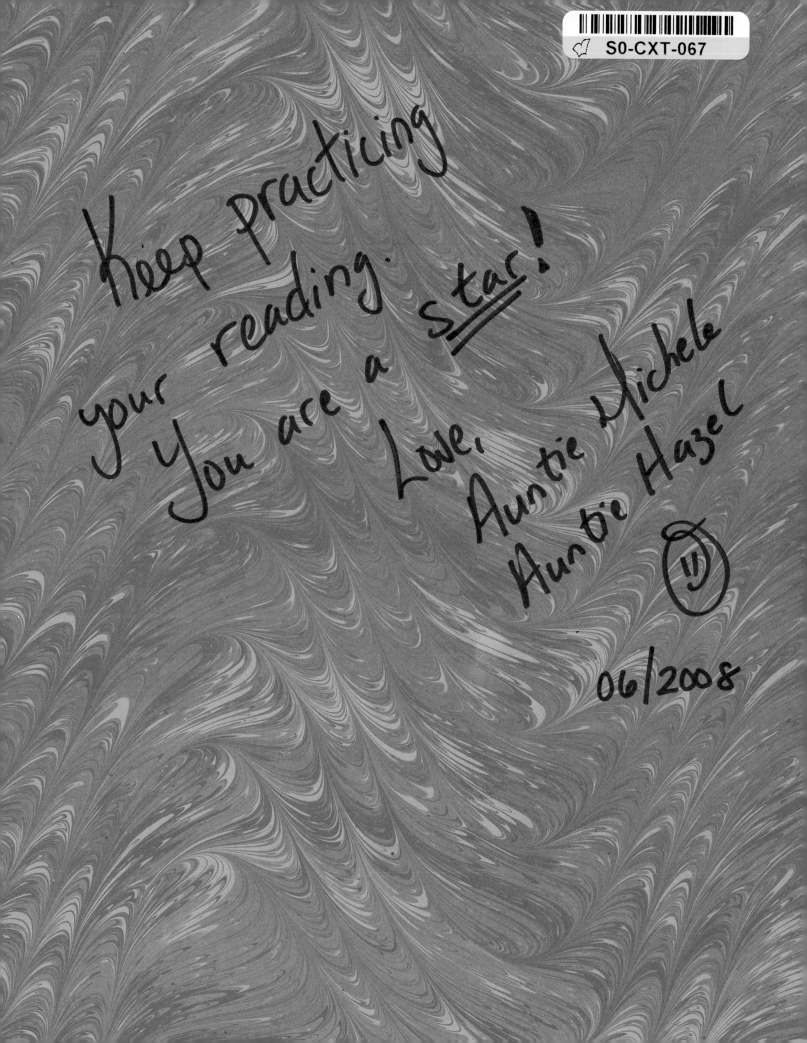

Keep practicing
your reading.
You are a star!

Love,
Auntie Michele
Auntie Hazel

06/2008

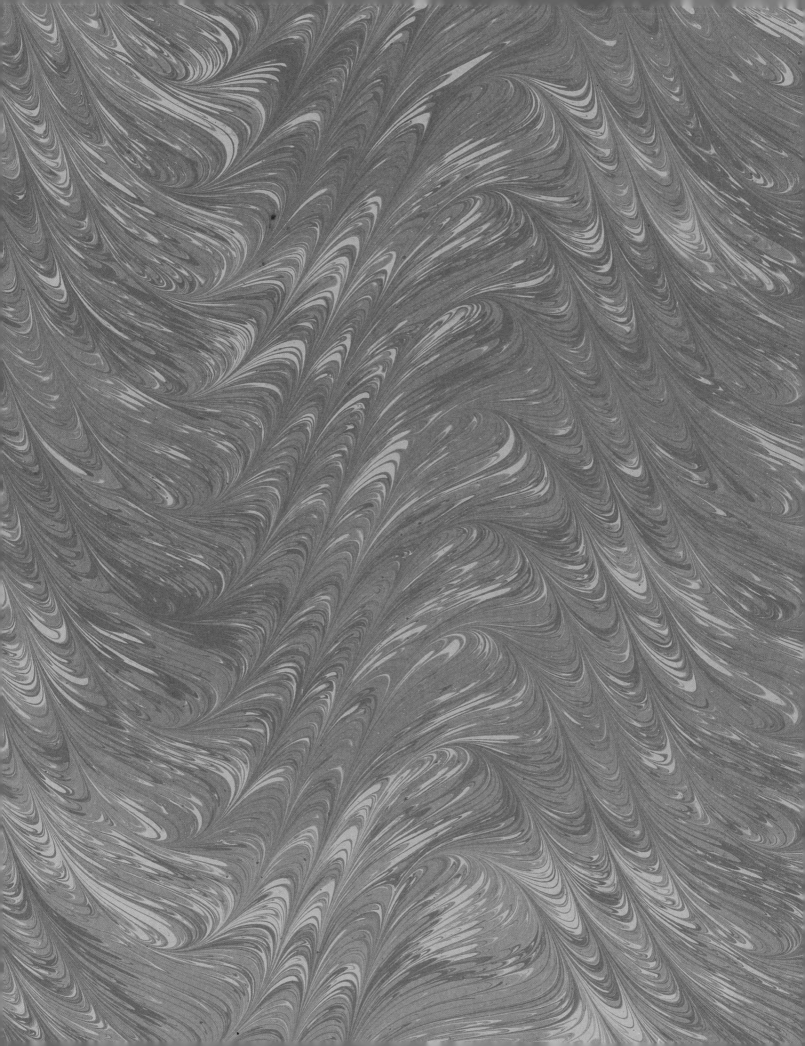

HARCOURT
· T R O P H I E S ·

A HARCOURT READING/LANGUAGE ARTS PROGRAM

GUESS WHO

SENIOR AUTHORS
Isabel L. Beck ◆ Roger C. Farr ◆ Dorothy S. Strickland

AUTHORS
Alma Flor Ada ◆ Marcia Brechtel ◆ Margaret McKeown
Nancy Roser ◆ Hallie Kay Yopp

SENIOR CONSULTANT
Asa G. Hilliard III

CONSULTANTS
F. Isabel Campoy ◆ David A. Monti

Harcourt

Orlando   Boston   Dallas   Chicago   San Diego

Visit *The Learning Site!*

www.harcourtschool.com

Requests for permission to make copies of any part of the work should be addressed to School Permissions and Copyrights, Harcourt, Inc., 6277 Sea Harbor Drive, Orlando, Florida 32887-6777. Fax: 407-345-2418.

HARCOURT and the Harcourt Logo are trademarks of Harcourt, Inc., registered in the United States of America and/or other jurisdictions.

Acknowledgments appear in the back of this book.

Printed in the United States of America

ISBN 0-15-326500-0

3 4 5 6 7 8 9 10 048 10 09 08 07 06 05 04 03 02

Dear Reader,

In **Guess Who,** there are lots of friends to meet. In the beginning, you will meet some playful kittens. In the middle, you will learn about some amazing animals. At the end, you will take a walk through a park and learn about a tasty treat. Come on and join the fun!

Sincerely,

The Authors

The Authors

I Am Your Friend

CONTENTS

Theme Big Books

Sometimes
by Keith Baker

All I Am
by Eileen Roe
illustrated by
Helen Cogancherry

Decodable Books 1-3

DECODABLE BOOK

5

Just for Fun

CONTENTS

Theme Big Books

Decodable Books 4-6

I Am
Your Friend

Word Power

Words to Remember

down

got

up

Pam **got** a hat.
Dan ran **up**.
Pam ran **down**.

Genre

Realistic Fiction

Realistic fiction stories sound like they could have happened, but they didn't.

Look for:

- characters that are people.

- places you have heard about or visited.

12

The Hat

by Holly Keller

Pam had a hat.

Pam ran up.

Pam ran down.

Dan ran up.

Dan ran down.

Dan got the hat!

Go, Dan!   Go, Pam!

Think and Respond

1. How does Pam lose her hat?

2. What does Pam do after she loses her hat?

3. How does Dan help Pam?

4. Would you like a friend like Dan? Why or why not?

5. What do you think Dan and Pam will do next?

Meet the Author/Illustrator
Holly Keller

Holly Keller likes to write about friends and their adventures. In "The Hat," Pam and Dan have quite an adventure when Pam's hat blows off. Holly Keller says, "It was great fun showing how Dan helps Pam. Good friends always help one another."

Holly Keller

Visit *The Learning Site!*
www.harcourtschool.com

23

Making Connections

Group Story

W ork in a group to make up another story about Dan and Pam. Tell your story to your classmates.

Listening/ Speaking CONNECTION

In the Wind

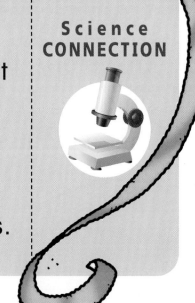

Science CONNECTION

Make a streamer out of paper or ribbon. On the next windy day, hold up your streamer. You can't see the wind, but the streamer will show you how the air moves.

Make a Hat

Art CONNECTION

Use colored paper to make your own hat. See if your hat will stay on when you're out in the wind!

25

Sequence

In a story, things have to happen in an order that makes sense. Look at these pictures from "The Hat."

What happened first?
What happened in the middle?
What happened at the end?

Test Prep
Sequence

> **Max**
>
> Max ran!
> Max had a nap.
> Dad got Max up.

I. **What did Max do first?**

- ○ Max got up.
- ○ Max ran.
- ○ Max had a nap.

Tip

Think about the order in which things happened. Read the story again if you can't remember.

▲ Sam and the Bag

Word Power

**Words to
Remember**

and

in

oh

yes

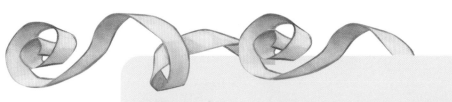

Sam ran up **and** down.
Oh, Sam!
Can you go **in** the bag?
Yes, you can!

Genre

Fiction

Fiction stories sound like they could have happened, but they didn't.

Look for:

- Characters you could see every day.

- Characters doing things they might really do.

Sam
and the
Bag

by Alison Jeffries
illustrated by Dan Andreasen

31

Max ran in the bag.

Hap ran in the bag.

Sam ran up the bag.

Sam ran down the bag.

Can Sam go in?

Yes, Sam can go in!

Oh, Sam!

Think and Respond

1. What do Max and Hap do at the beginning of the story?

2. What does Sam do when the other cats are in the bag?

3. What happens when Sam jumps into the bag?

4. Do you think Max and Hap will let Sam play with them again? Why or why not?

5. What do you think Sam learns?

Meet the Illustrator
Dan Andreasen

When Dan Andreasen's daughter was in kindergarten, her teacher asked, "What does your Daddy do?" His daughter said, "He colors!"

For "Sam and the Bag," he drew sketches of the pictures first. He covered the background with a color called burnt sienna to give a special glow. Then he used oil paints.

Kittens

by Charles Ghigna

illustrated by Cary Phillips

Curled up in
A ball of fur,
Kittens mew,
Kittens purr.

Kittens like to
Climb and see
All the birds
Up in the tree.

Kittens tumble.
Kittens play,
Inside outside
Every day.

Making Connections

How Many Cats?

Sam is little. Max and Hap are bigger. Draw two big cats and one little cat. How many cats did you draw?

Math CONNECTION

44

When I'm Bigger

Soon Sam will be bigger. What will you be like when you are bigger? Draw and write about being bigger. Share your work.

Acting Sam

Make a finger puppet of Sam. Use it to act out the story. Take it off when Sam jumps into the bag.

Short Vowel a

The letter **a** can stand for the /a/ sound. Say <u>cat</u>. The /a/ sound is the short sound of **a**.

Name these pictures. Which one does **not** have the short sound of **a** in the middle?

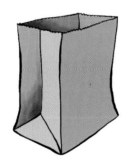

Say <u>Sam</u>, <u>Max</u>, and <u>Hap</u>. What sound do you hear in the middle?

Test Prep
Short Vowel a

1. Which picture name has the short sound of a?

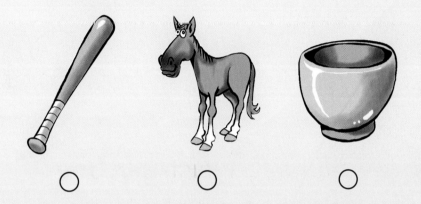

○　　　　○　　　　○

2. Which picture name has the short sound of a?

○　　　　○　　　　○

Tip

Say /a/. Then say a picture name. Does the picture name have the /a/ sound?

▲ Ants

Word Power

Words to Remember

make

they

walk

Can ants **walk**?
What can **they make**?
You will see!

49

Nonfiction

A nonfiction story tells about things that are real.

Look for:

- **Things that you see in the real world.**

- **Real photographs of animals such as ants.**

Ants

by Jonathan Zea

Look at the big hill.

What is in it?

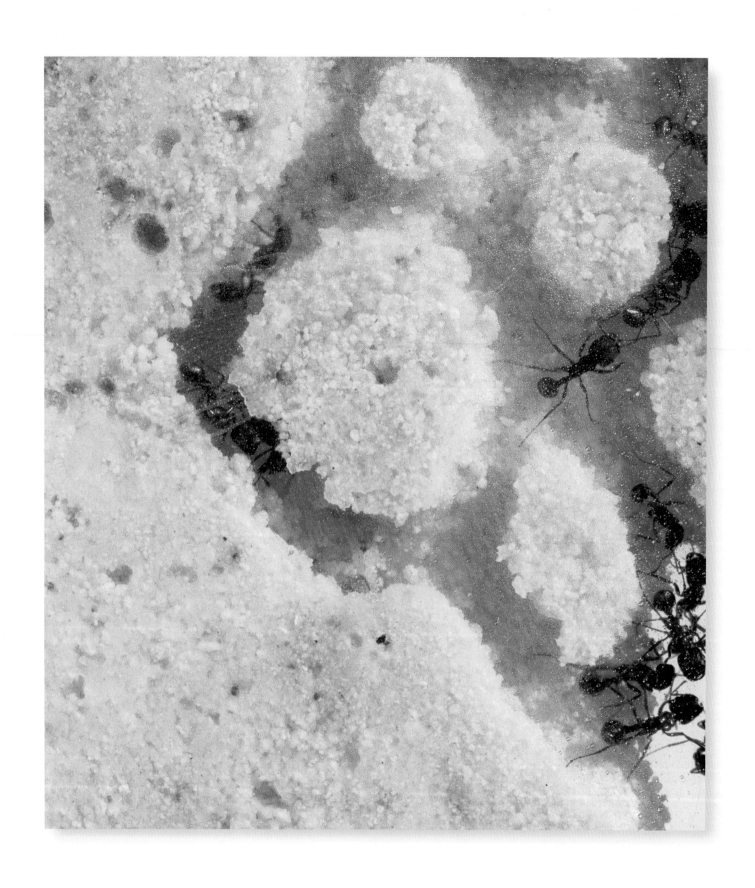

Ants!

Ants make big homes.

They walk and walk.

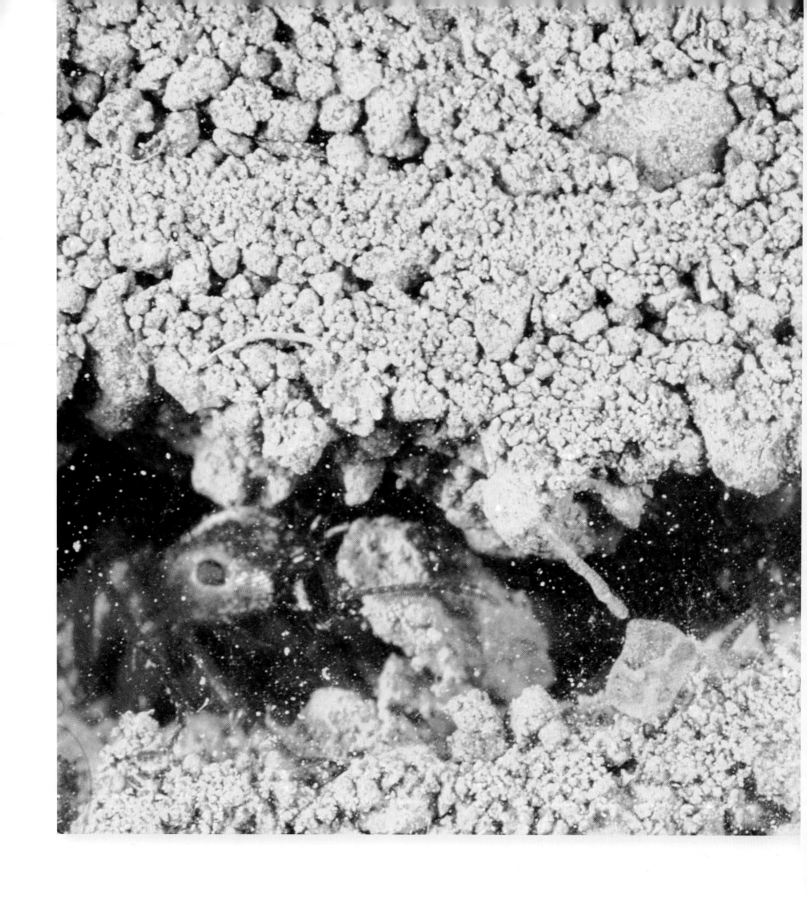

They dig and dig.

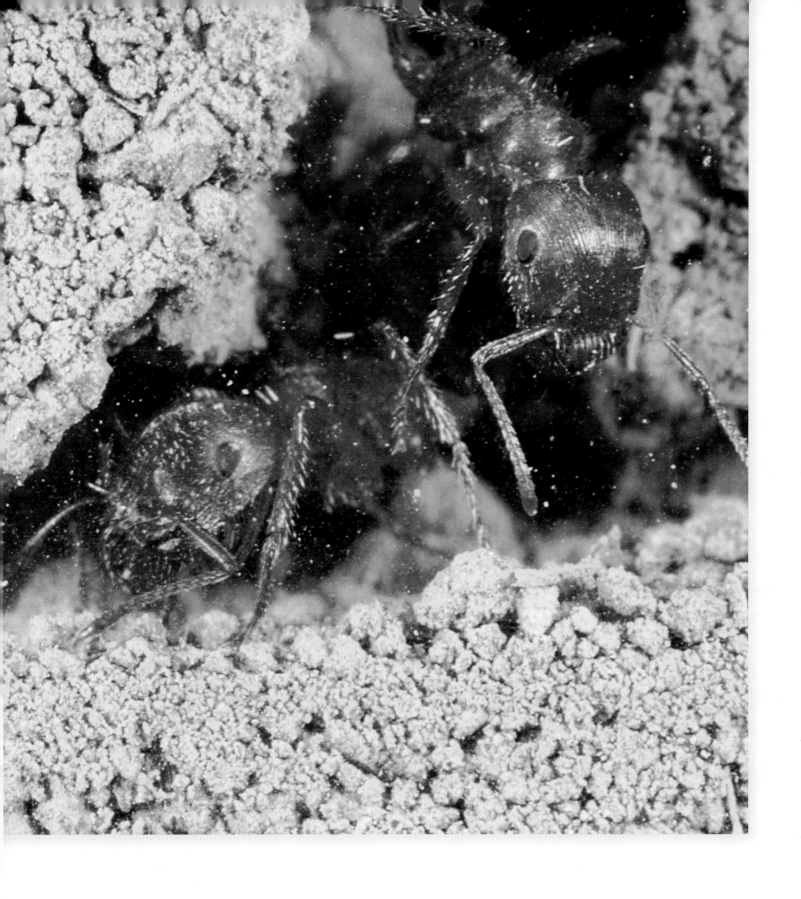

They lift and lift.

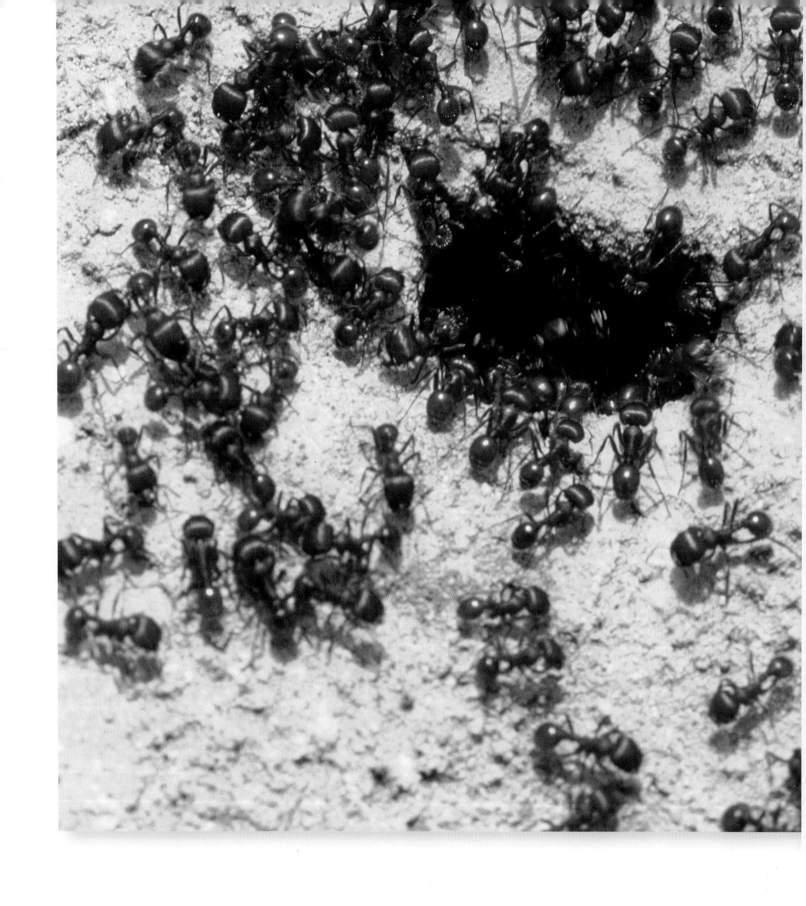

Ants go in the hill.

Think and Respond

1 What did you see the ants do?

2 Ants do many of the same things people do. Name some of these things.

3 What is an ant's home made of?

4 Do you think ants are hard workers? Explain.

5 If you were an ant, which job would you like best? Why?

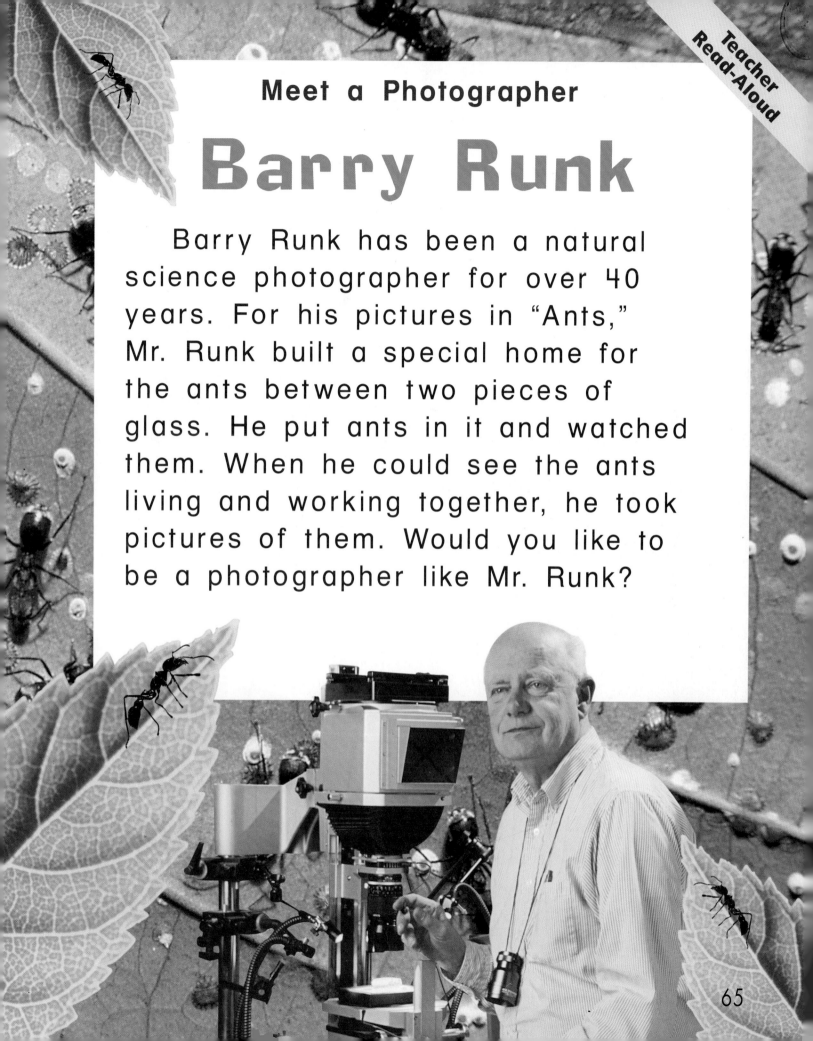

Meet a Photographer

Barry Runk

Barry Runk has been a natural science photographer for over 40 years. For his pictures in "Ants," Mr. Runk built a special home for the ants between two pieces of glass. He put ants in it and watched them. When he could see the ants living and working together, he took pictures of them. Would you like to be a photographer like Mr. Runk?

Making Connections

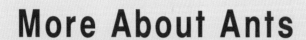

More About Ants

Ants are very interesting. Find out two new things about ants. Share what you learn.

Science/Technology CONNECTION

Just Like Us

Ants and people do some of the same things. Draw an ant digging or lifting something. Then draw yourself doing that, too.

Social Studies CONNECTION

Ants Work Together

Draw and write about ants doing something together. Your story can be real or make-believe.

Writing CONNECTION

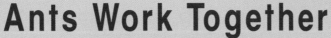

Details

When you read a story, you don't need to remember all the small things, or **details**. You do need to remember the important details so you can understand what you read.

Read this part of the story "Ants."

Ants make big homes.
They dig and dig.

- **What do ants make?**
- **How do they do this?**

Test Prep
Details

The Ants

The ants ran up the hill.
They got food and milk.
The ants ran down.

I. **What did the ants get?**

○ They got a hill.

○ They got food and milk.

○ They got a lamp.

Read carefully. Think about why the ants went up the hill.

69

Just for Fun

71

▲ Jack and Rick

Word Power

Words to
Remember

help

now

play

too

want

I **want** to **play**.
I **want** you to **play**, **too**.
Can you **play now**?
I can **help** you.

Genre

Fantasy

A fantasy is a story about something that could never happen.

Look for:

- **Animal characters that act like people.**

74

Jack and Rick

by David McPhail

Jack and Rick want to play.

Can Jack pick up the log?

No! It's too big!

Can Rick help Jack?

Yes! Rick can pass the rope.

Can they lift it now?

Yes, they can!

Can Rick walk to Jack?

No! Oh, no!

Can Jack help Rick?

Yes, Jack can help.

Now Jack and Rick can play!

Think and Respond

1 Where are Jack and Rick at the beginning of the story?

2 Why can't Jack pick up the log?

3 How do Jack and Rick move the log?

4 What does the author tell us about working together?

5 Which part of the story do you think is the funniest? Why?

Meet the Author
David McPhail

David McPhail loves to put words and pictures together to make stories. He says, "I like the way the characters find a way to get on the same side of the stream—even though it's not easy." He hopes you help your friends the way Rick and Jack helped each other!

David McPhail

89

Bridges Th

People have always
needed bridges.

Long ago, bridges
looked like this.

Today, many bridges
look like this.

Bridges bring
people together.

Making Connections

More Adventures

Talk about other things Jack and Rick could do by working together. Choose one idea. Write a sentence to share.

Writing CONNECTION

92

Real Workers

Find pictures of people working together. Make a poster showing different jobs.

Social Studies CONNECTION

People Working Together

Beavers Working Together

Beavers work together to make homes and dams. Find out something about beavers. Share what you learn.

Science CONNECTION

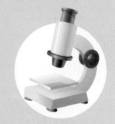

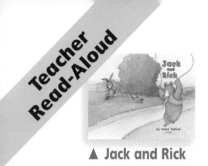
Sequence

In a story, things happen in an order that makes sense. Look at these pictures from "Jack and Rick."

What happens first?
What happens next?
What happens last?

Test Prep
Sequence

Mack

Mack got up to bat.
Mack had a hit!
Mack ran fast.

1. **What did Mack do last?**
   ○ Mack hit.
   ○ Mack ran.
   ○ Mack got up
      to bat.

Tip

If you forget
what happened
last, read the
sentences
again.

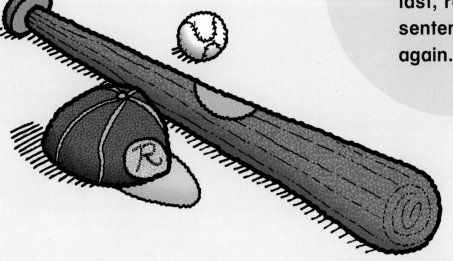

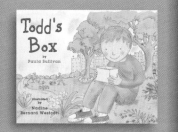

▲ Todd's Box

Word Power

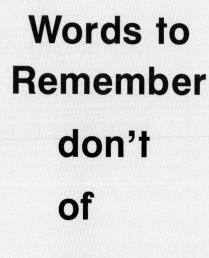

Words to Remember

don't

of

so

The box is **so** little.
Is it a box **of** rocks?
Don't look in it now!

Realistic Fiction

Realistic fiction stories sound like they could have happened, but they didn't.

Look for:

- Characters who are people.
- Events that are like things you have done or seen.

Todd's Box

by

Paula Sullivan

illustrated by

Nadine Bernard Westcott

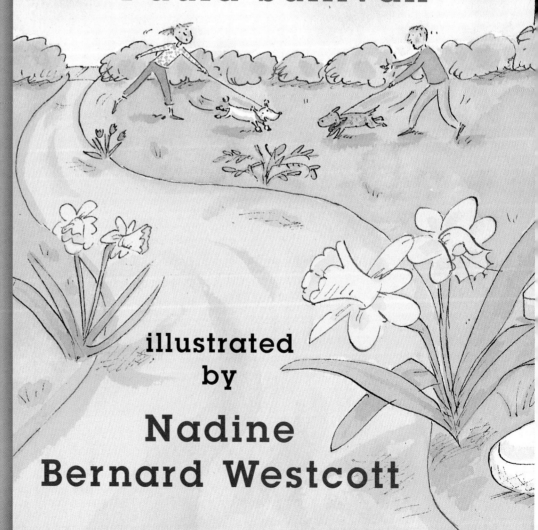

Look, Mom!
I can dig in the sand.

Not now, Todd.

Look, Mom!
I am on the rocks.

Hop off, Todd.

Look, Mom!
The ant is so fast.

Don't pick it up, Todd.

Look, Mom!
It's a pond.

We have to go, Todd.

Look, Mom!
Here's a gift for you.

Look in and see.

Oh, Todd!
It's a box of surprises!

Think and Respond

1 How does Todd surprise his mom?

2 Why is Todd's mom so surprised?

3 What do you think Todd's mom learns in this story?

4 Tell about a time you picked things up on a walk like Todd's.

5 Why does Todd say "Look, Mom!" so many times?

Nadine Bernard Westcott

Meet the Illustrator

Nadine Bernard Westcott

Nadine Bernard Westcott started to draw when she was very young. She likes to draw pictures for children because she says it's fun!

For "Todd's Box," she drew the pictures with a special black pen. Then she painted the pictures. She thought bright pastel colors would be good for the story. How do her pictures make you feel?

113

Making Connections

A Class Walk

Take a walk with your group in the schoolyard. Make a list of things you see and hear.

Science **CONNECTION**

Things I See and Hear

birds
rocks

A Nice Gift

Todd gave his mother a gift. What gift would you like to give a family member? Draw a picture of your gift. Write about it.

Writing CONNECTION

I would like to give flowers to my Grandma.

How Many?

Put some things into a box. Count them with a partner. Then write this sentence on a sheet of paper. Fill in the number.

Math CONNECTION

We have _____ things in the box.

▲ Todd's Box

Short Vowel o

The letter **o** can stand for the /o/ sound. This is the sound you hear in <u>Todd</u>. This is the short sound of **o**.

Which picture below does <u>not</u> have the short sound of **o** in the middle?

Name these pictures. What sound do you hear in the middle?

Test Prep
Short o

1. Which picture name has the short sound of <u>o</u>?

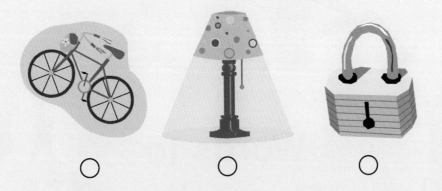

○   ○   ○

2. Which picture name has the short sound of <u>o</u>?

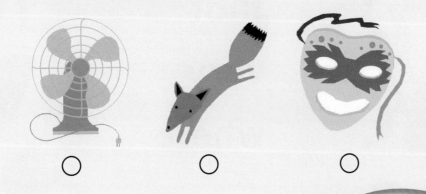

○   ○   ○

Tip

Say /o/. Then say a picture name. Does the picture name have the /o/ sound?

117

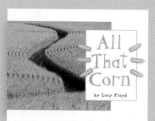

Word Power

Words to
Remember

buy

that

very

where

Look at all **that** corn!
It looks **very** big.
Where did you **buy** it?
I want to **buy** corn like
that!

119

Nonfiction

Nonfiction describes books of information and fact.

Look for:

- Photographs that help explain.

- Information about one topic.

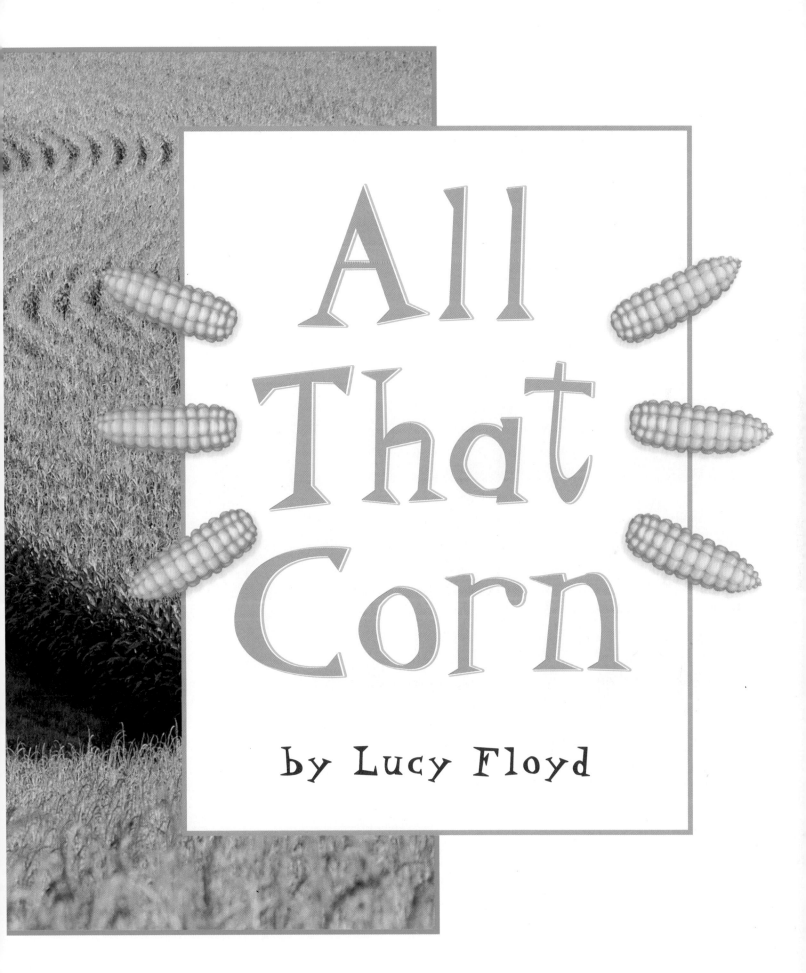

All That Corn

by Lucy Floyd

Look at all **that** corn!

It's very tall!
It's as tall as a wall!

Pick! Pick! Pick!
Pick all the corn.

Where will the corn go?

Here it is.
The corn is in cans.

Where will the corn go?

Here it is.
We can buy corn at the store.

Where will it go now?

Here it is.
The corn is at home.

Where will it go now?

Here it is.
Pop! Pop! Pop!

Look at all that corn!

Think and Respond

1. How does corn get to your home?

2. Why do farmers pick corn with machines?

3. Why does the author say that the corn is "as tall as a wall"?

4. What kind of corn is the family eating?

5. What is your favorite way to eat corn?

Meet the Author
Lucy Floyd

When Lucy Floyd was a child, she saw cornfields when she visited her grandmother. She says, "I wrote about corn because I love popcorn! I think most children do, too."

Lucy Floyd

Popalong Hopcorn!

by Judith Nicholls

illustrated by Buket Erdogen

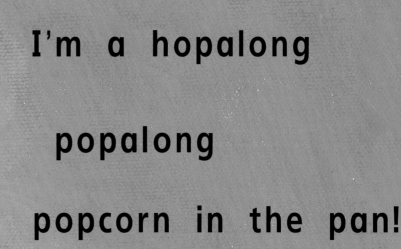

I'm a hopalong

popalong

popcorn in the pan!

In

out

up

down!

Catch me

if

you

can!

Making Connections

Healthful Snacks

Popcorn is a good snack. What are some others? Make a poster. Show snacks that are good for you.

Health CONNECTION

Snacks That Are Good for You

138

Busy Workers

There are many workers in "All That Corn." Make a list of the workers. Draw what they do.

As Tall as a Wall

The author says the corn is as tall as a wall. Finish this sentence. Draw a picture to go with it.

It's as big as a _____.

It's as big as a house.

Sequence

You know that in a story, things must happen in an order that makes sense. Look at these pictures from "All That Corn."

- **What happens first?**
- **What happens next?**
- **What happens last?**

Test Prep
Sequence

A Trip to the Store

We walk to the store.
We buy a can of corn.
We walk back home.

1. What do we do first?

○ We go home.

○ We go to the store.

○ We buy the corn.

Tip

Think about the order of the story. What must you do before you can buy the corn?

Words for Writing

People Words

baby

boy

doctor

girl

mail carrier

man

police officer

teacher

woman

Color Words

black

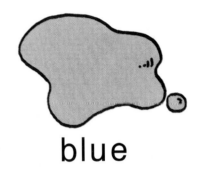

blue

brown

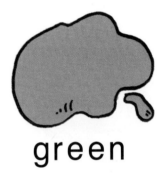

green

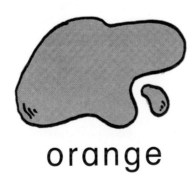

orange

purple

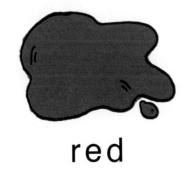

red

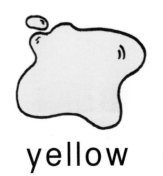

yellow

Words for Writing

Number Words

1 one

2 two

3 three

4 four

5 five

6 six

7 seven

8 eight

9 nine

Shape Words

circle

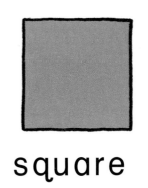

square

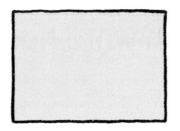

rectangle

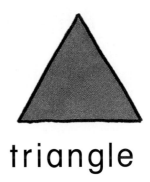

triangle

star

heart

Glossary

What is a Glossary?

A glossary can help you read a word. You can look up the word and read it in a sentence. Each word has a picture to help you.

gift Jill got a **gift**.

ants   **Ants** are small bugs.

bag   I have a **bag** of corn.

dig   We can **dig** in the sand.

gift   Jill got a **gift**.

hat   Tom's **hat** is red.

help   Can you **help** me get up?

hill   The dog ran up the **hill**.

hop   Ben can **hop** on one leg.

play   The cat can **play** with the ball.

pond   The **pond** is full of fish.

rocks   Spot rests on the **rocks**.

tall   My dad is **tall**.

walk   Little Pam can **walk**.

wall   The pup is on the **wall**.

Acknowledgments

For permission to reprint copyrighted material, grateful acknowledgment is made to the following sources:

Charles Ghigna: "Kittens" from *Animal Trunk: Silly Poems to Read Aloud* by Charles Ghigna. Text copyright © 1999 by Charles Ghigna.
Judith Nicholls: "Popalong Hopcorn!" from *Popcorn Pie* by Judith Nicholls. Text copyright © 1988 by Judith Nicholls.

Photo Credits

Key: (t) = top; (b) = bottom; (c) = center; (l) = left; (r) = right.
Page 23, Tom Sobolik / Black Star; 41, Mike Steinberg / Black Star; 48-49, Darren Robb / Stone; 49, Tim Flach / Stone; 50-51, Gary Retherford / Photo Researchers, Inc.; 50-51(leaves), Tim Flach / Stone; 50, Gary Retherford / Photo Researchers, Inc.; 52-53, Rob & Ann Simpson / Visuals Unlimited; 54-55, Runk / Schoenberger / Grant Heilman Photography; 56-57, Darren Robb / Stone; 58-59, Runk / Schoenberger / Grant Heilman Photography; 60-61, Gary Bumgarner / Stone; 62-63, P. Burd / H. Armstrong Roberts; 64-65, Kjell B. Sandved / Visuals Unlimited; 64-65(leaves), Tim Flach / Stone; 65, Grant Heilman Photography; 66, Charles Krebs / Stone; 68(tl), Gary Retherford / Photo Researchers, Inc.; 68(tr), Rob & Ann Simpson / Visuals Unlimited; 68(cr), 68(br), Runk / Schoenberger / Grant Heilman Photography; 89, Rick Friedman / Black Star; 90(t), Tom McHugh / Photo Researchers, Inc.; 90(b), Robert Maier / Earth Scenes; 91(t), 91(b), Superstock; 112, Rick Friedman / Black Star; 118(t), Denny Eilers / Grant Heilman Photography; 118(b), Runk / Schoenberger / Grant Heilman Photography; 119(t), Doug Dukane; 119(b), Maximilian Stock Ltd. / Earth Scenes; 120(t), Maximilian Stock Ltd. / Earth Scenes; 120-121, Denny Eilers / Grant Heilman Photography; 122, Zane Williams / Stone; 123, Michael Busselle / Stone; 123(inset), Ken Kinzie / Harcourt; 124, John Colwell / Grant Heilman Photography; 125, Lowell J. Georgia / Photo Researchers, Inc.; 126, H. Armstrong Roberts; 127, Alexander Lowry / Photo Researchers, Inc.; 127(corn), Maximilian Stock Ltd. / Earth Scenes; 128-133, Doug Dukane; 135, Rick Friedman / Black Star; 138, Denny Eilers / Grant Heilman Photography; 140(tl), Denny Eilers / Grant Heilman Photography; 140(tr), 140(bl), Doug Dukane; 140(br), John Colwell / Grant Heilman Photography; 146, Ken Kinzie / Harcourt; 147, Raymond A. Mendez / Animals Animals; 148(t), Superstock; 148(b), Ken Kinzie / Harcourt; 150, Superstock; 151, Jane Howard / Photo Researchers, Inc.; 152(t), Ulrike Welsch / Photo Researchers, Inc.; 152(b), LWA/Dann Tardif / Corbis Stock Market; 153, Norbert Schufer / Corbis Stock Market.

Illustration Credits

Richard Bernal, Cover Art; Dominic Catalano, 4-5, 8-9; Hala Wittwer, 6-7, 70-71; Holly Keller, 12-23; C. D. Hullinger, 24-25, 95; Alissa Imre Geis, 27, 66-67; Dan Andreasen, 30-41; Cary Phillips, 42-43; Clare Schaumann, 44-45; Eldon Doty, 47; John Hovell, 69; David McPhail, 74-89; Christine Mau, 92-93; Tom Leonard, 93; Nadine Bernard Westcott, 98-113; Steve Björkman, 114-115, 138-139; Buket Erdogen, 136-137; Steve Haskamp, 141.

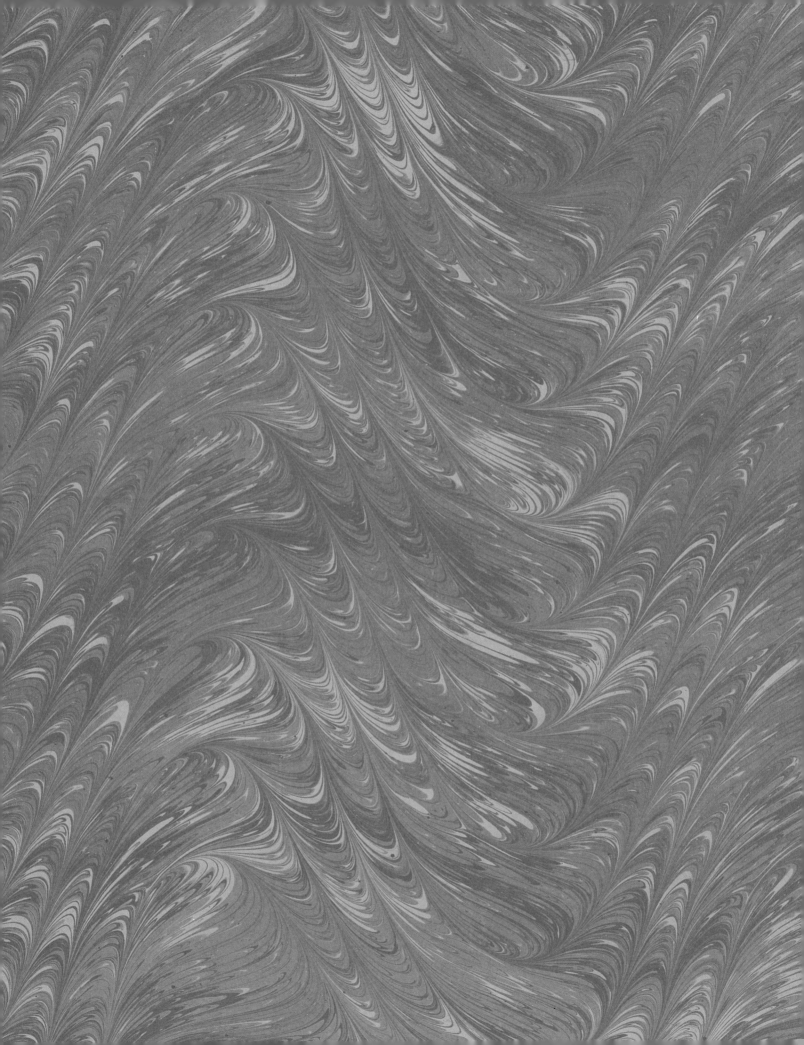

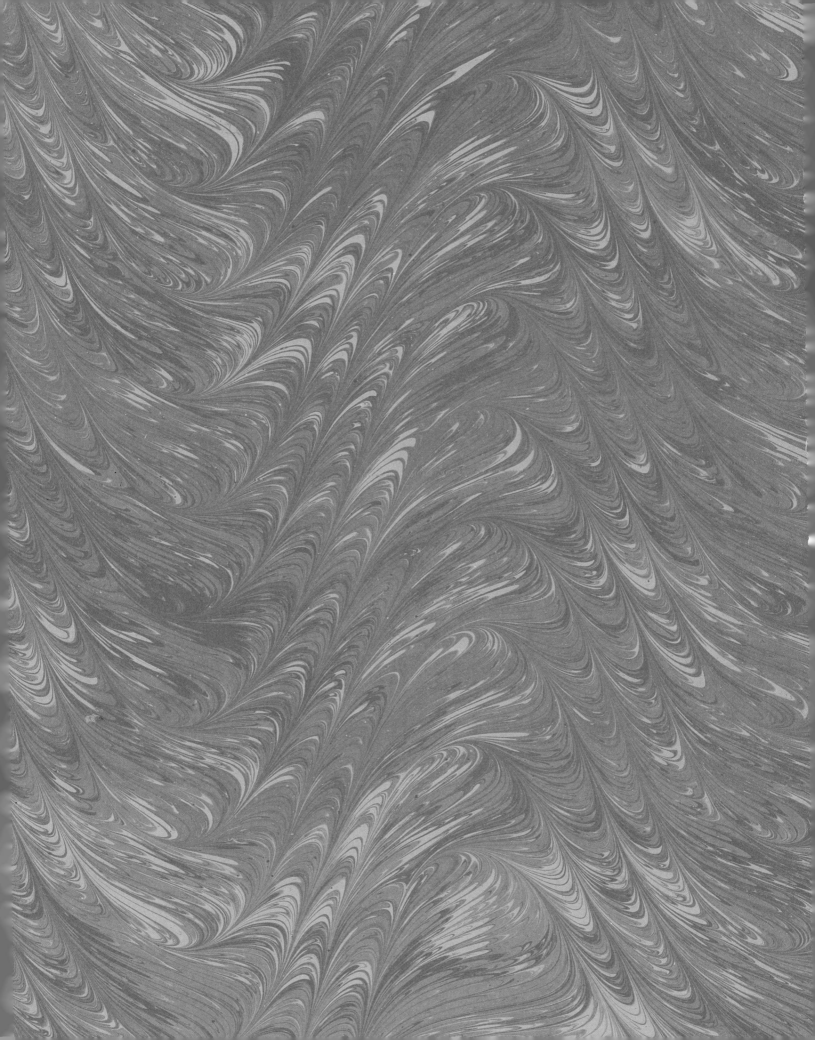